JESUS CHRIST IS LORD

THE BLOOD OF JESUS CHRIST

IN
SPIRITUAL WARFARE

**SERVANT OF THE LORD
ANDRE NGAMBU**

The Blood of Jesus Christ

DO NOT MEMORISE PRAYERS, BUT LEARN HOW TO PRAY.

www.planetberée.com

The Blood of Jesus Christ

Spiritual warfare request:

- A spiritual wisdom, the wisdom from above

-A spiritual strength, the strength of the Lord

-and spiritual weapons, armor of God.

The blood of Jesus Christ is one of these weapons

ISBN 978-1547262700

Copyright© 2017 Planet Berée
Tout droit de reproduction, de traduction et d'adaptations
réservées pour tous pays

**SERVITEUR DE L'ETERNEL
ANDRE NGAMBU**

Unless otherwise indicated, all Bible verses are taken from the Bible in the New International Version (NIV).

www.planetberee.com

Contents

Preface by the Author. 7
Introduction 9

   I. THE BLOOD OF JESUS CHRIST AND ITS
      FUNCTIONS....………………………..............11

  II. APPLY THE BLOOD OF JESUS CHRIST IN
      EVERYDAY LIFE. 18
      A. AT NIGHT
      B. IN THE MORNING
      C. BEFORE EATING
      D. THE BLOOD OF JESUS CHRIST IN EVERYDAY
      BATTLE

The Blood of Jesus Christ

Preface by the Author

I dedicate this book to the Almighty God who inspired me by his holy spirit to write this manual that will help many people on how to protect their lives and keep their deliverances.

I thank God for my biological mother "Helene Ma Wete" who had trained me to follow and love the Lord Jesus Christ.

I thank the Almighty God for my wife "Maman Grace" who never ceases to intercede for me and the whole family.

I can never forget anyone who contributes from near or from far with encouragement and comments that encourages me to go deeper into prayer and seek for what we need to continue serving you and that together we continue to win Victories over victories, and that we are strengthened to keep our deliverance.

Through the shedding of Jesus Christ, God has reconciled us with him and peace now reigns between our God and the sinner.

The Blood of Jesus Christ

The Blood of Jesus Christ
Introduction

In spiritual warfare, the Blood of Jesus Christ is a very powerful weapon that gives us victory over satan and all his acolytes.

It is both an offensive and defensive weapon.

We have a lot of authority before satan and his henchmen when we declare that "Satan is defeated by the blood of Jesus Christ" and to this all his accusations lose power.

The Word of God declares:

Revelation 12:11 they triumphed over him because of the blood of the Lamb, and because of the word of their testimony, and they did not love their lives until they feared death.

We will win this victory only when we decide to live in the certainties gained by the work accomplished at the cross by the Lord Jesus Christ.

Therefore, faith must be fully active in our lives.

Does your prayer life reflect the kind of relationship you have with God through the blood of His Son?

In this manual you will learn how and when to use the blood of Jesus Christ in different circumstances of your daily life in order to find divine protection.

The Blood of Jesus Christ

The Blood of Jesus Christ

I. THE BLOOD OF JESUS CHRIST AND ITS FUNCTIONS

In the Old Testament the children of Israel needed a sacrifice of atonement and it was the blood of animals that was shed for sin to be atoned, that is, covered. With the Atonement, God no longer saw the sin that was covered, but the blood that had expiated it (covered)

In the New Testament, on the cross, Jesus Christ became our sacrifice, our Savior...

For his blood alone expiated our sins.

Hebrews 10:3-4
³ But those sacrifices are an annual reminder of sins.
⁴ It is impossible for the blood of bulls and goats to take away sins.

The Blood of Jesus Christ performs many functions in our lives:

A) The blood of Jesus Christ delivers us from our sins.

The word of God declares:
Revelation 1:5-6
⁵ ...To him who loves us and has freed us from our sins by his blood,
⁶ and has made us to be a kingdom and priests to serve

his God and Father—to him be glory and power for ever and ever! Amen.

The Word of God declares:

Ephesians 1:7
⁷ In him we have redemption through his blood, the forgiveness of sins, in accordance with the riches of God's grace

Thanks to the blood of Jesus, our sins are forgiven.

Matthew 26:28.
For this is my blood, the blood of the covenant, which is poured out for many, for the remission of sins.

B) The Blood of Jesus Christ sanctifies
Hebrews 13:12
That is why Jesus also, in order to sanctify the people by his own blood, suffered outside the city gate.

C) The Blood of Jesus Christ purifies us.

The purifying power of the Blood of Jesus Christ purifies us from all sin.

The word of God declares;
1 John 1:7
But if we walk in the light, as he is in the light, we have fellowship with one another, and the blood of Jesus, his Son, purifies us from all sin.

The blood of Jesus Christ purifies our consciousness of dead works so that we serve the living God.

Hebrews 9:14
[14] How much more, then, will the blood of Christ, who through the eternal Spirit offered himself unblemished to God, cleanse our consciences from acts that lead to death,[a] so that we may serve the living God!

D) The Blood of Jesus Christ justifies us

* The Word of God declares:
Romans 8:33
We are justified by the blood of Jesus Christ, from the day when God accepted the blood of his son as the only way to forgive our sins.

Romans 5: 9
Since we have now been justified by His Blood, how much more shall we be saved from God's wrath through Him.

E) The blood of Jesus Christ is the means by which Jesus Christ redeemed the Church.

The Blood of Jesus Christ

1 Peter 1: 18-19
18 For you know that it was not with perishable things such as silver or gold that you were redeemed from the vain way of life which you inherited from your ancestors,
19 but by the precious blood of Christ, as of a lamb without blemish and without defect,

Revelation 5: 9
And they sang a new song, saying, you are worthy to take the book, and to open its seals; because you were slain, and you have redeemed for God by your blood men of every tribe, tongue, nation, and nation;

Acts 20:28
[28] Keep watch over yourselves and all the flock of which the Holy Spirit has made you overseers. Be shepherds of the church of God, which he bought with his own blood.

F) It is through the Blood of Jesus Christ that we have access to the holy place.

Hebrews 10:19-22
[19] Therefore, brothers and sisters, since we have confidence to enter the Most Holy Place by the blood of Jesus,
[20] by a new and living way opened for us through the curtain, that is, his body,
[21] and since we have a great priest over the house of

God,
²² let us draw near to God with a sincere heart and with the full assurance that faith brings, having our hearts sprinkled to cleanse us from a guilty conscience and having our bodies washed with pure water.

Mark 15:38
It is the Blood that gives us access to the Father's throne; "The curtain of the temple was torn in two from top to bottom."

John 6:54
Whoever eats my flesh and drinks my blood has eternal life, and I will raise them up at the last day.

G) The Blood of Jesus Christ heals both the soul and the body.

The blood of Jesus gives life to those who consume it.

The blood of Jesus allows us to dwell in Jesus Christ, to be in communion with Him.

John 6:53
Jesus said to them, "Jesus said to them, "Very truly I tell you, unless you eat the flesh of the Son of Man and drink his blood, you have no life in you.

John 6: 56
Whoever eats my flesh and drinks my blood remains in me, and I in them.

H) The Blood of Jesus Christ is the foundation of the new covenant. It is a Blood that brings together Jews and pagans

The blood of Jesus Christ gives us peace and reconciles us with God.

Colossians 1:20.
and through him to reconcile to himself all things, whether things on earth or things in heaven, by making peace through his blood, shed on the cross.

Matthew 26:28
for this is my blood, the blood of the covenant, which is poured out for many, for the remission of sins.

1 Corinthians 11:25
And after supper, he took the cup, and said, this cup is the new covenant in my blood; Do this in memory of me whenever you drink it.

Luke 22:20
And he took the cup after supper, and gave it to them, saying, this cup is the new covenant in my blood, which is poured out for you.

Ephesians 2:13
But now in Christ Jesus, you who were formerly distant, you were brought near by the blood of Christ.

I) The Blood of Jesus Christ protects us from all danger

Exodus 12:13
The blood shall serve you as a sign upon the houses where you are; I will see the blood, and I will pass over you, and there shall be no plague which destroys you, when I strike the land of Egypt.

J) The blood of Jesus pleads in our favor in heaven before the throne of God.

Hebrews 12: 22-24
[22] But you have come to Mount Zion, to the city of the living God, the heavenly Jerusalem. You have come to thousands upon thousands of angels in joyful assembly, [23] to the church of the firstborn, whose names are written in heaven. You have come to God, the Judge of all, to the spirits of the righteous made perfect, [24] to Jesus the mediator of a new covenant, and to the sprinkled blood that speaks a better word than the blood of Abel.

I. APPLY THE BLOOD OF JESUS CHRIST IN EVERYDAY LIFE.

AT NIGHT,
In the night, evil men and women gather to attack, destroy and steal human lives.
The Word of God declares:
Matthew 13:25
But while everyone was sleeping, his enemy came and sowed weeds among the wheat, and went away.

In the night wicked men and women, sow tares in human lives, exchange blessings into curses, establish satanic pacts and decrees.

I) Apply the Blood of Jesus Christ for protection:
- against nightly agitators, changers of blessings.
– Against people who cast bad spells, who pronounce curses on human lives.

ii) Apply the blood of Jesus Christ to destroy sites where evil men and women gather in the night.

iii) Apply the blood of Jesus Christ against any physical or spiritual being that sows tares in human lives during the night.

iv) Apply the blood of Jesus Christ to neutralize the effects of any physical or spiritual food or beverage poisoned diabolically by Satan and his agents.

v) Apply the blood of Jesus Christ in your home to prevent any diabolical entry or exit from humans, animals or anything else.

vi) Soak your life and your whole family into the blood of Jesus Christ so that the enemy cannot see or touch you.

The Word of God declares: **Psalm 91: 4-5 4**
He shall cover thee with his feathers, and thou shalt find refuge under his wings; His fidelity is a shield and a cuirass. 5 Thou shalt not be afraid of the terrors of the night, nor of the arrow that flies by day,

1. I plead the Blood of Jesus Christ, to render void and ineffectual all satanic decrees in heaven, all the decrees of witchcraft, and all enchantment made day and night against me, my wife (husband) And all our children, in the name of Jesus Christ.

2. The Word of God declares:
Psalm 18:14
He shot his arrows and scattered the enemy, with great bolts of lightning he routed them.

3. Let the blood of Jesus Christ flows into streams, rivers, seas and oceans all over the world to swallow up all the agents of darkness that gathering or planning to come together to invoke my name, the name of my wife (my husband) And of my children, in the name of Jesus Christ.

4. I apply the blood of Jesus Christ on every road that the sorcerers use to reach us, that it may become slippery and dark, in the name of Jesus Christ.

5. The Word of God declares;
Isaiah 54:17
no weapon forged against you will prevail, and you will refute every tongue that accuses you.
This is the heritage of the servants of the LORD, and this is their vindication from me, "declares the LORD.

6. I apply the blood of Jesus Christ all around our plot on earth and in the air, that no one, no animal or any other satanic device would be able to trespass our limits, in the name of Jesus Christ.

7. I apply the blood of Jesus Christ on the doors, windows, concretes and any other means that devil agents use or can use to enter my house that the enemy cannot approach of these ways, in the name of Jesus Christ.

8. **Leviticus 26: 6**
"'I will grant peace in the land, and you will lie down and no one will make you afraid. I will remove wild beasts from the land, and the sword will not pass through your country.

9. Let the blood of Jesus Christ be sprinkled in every part of our house, on every object in our house to dislodge any spirit of Morpheus assigned by the world of darkness to exchange my blessings to curses in our dreams, in the name of Jesus Christ.

10. Let the blood of Jesus Christ affects the functioning of all mystical radars and cameras placed around / or in our homes, in the name of Jesus Christ.

11. **Psalm 91:10**
no harm will overtake you, no disaster will come near your tent.

12. Let the power that is in the blood of Jesus Christ overthrows and annihilates all power of the world of

darkness working against me, in the name of Jesus Christ.

13. Let all arrows of evil spells that are cast or prepared to be cast upon us during our sleep, be destroyed and broken by the power of Jesus Christ' blood.

14. The Bible declares; He annihilated the plans of the cunning men, therefore, let the blood of Jesus Christ annihilated every project by the enemy to introduce the spirit husband or woman into my household, in the name of Jesus Christ.

15. Any person or spirit received mission to implant demonic objects in my system or in that of my wife and all our children in dreams, be struck, in the name of Jesus Christ.

Proverbs 3:24
When you lie down, you will not be afraid; when you lie down; your sleep will be sweet.

17. I lie down and go to sleep in peace, for the LORD hath given me security in my dwelling. Psalms 4:9

18. Let the blood of Jesus Christ cover my children during their sleep and that, their sleep be sweet.

19. Let he blood of Jesus Christ paralyzes every animal or spirit that brings evil dreams into my sleep, in the name of Jesus Christ.

The word of God declares; **Job 33: 14-16**
[14] God speaks, however, sometimes in one way, sometimes in another, and we do not take care.
[15] He speaks by dreams, by nocturnal visions, when men are given up to a deep sleep, when they are asleep on their beds.
[16] So he gives them warnings and puts the seal to his instructions,

20. I plead the blood of Jesus Christ to reveal every face veiled or concealed behind another representation to deceive us of its true identity in the name of Jesus Christ.

21. Let the blood of Jesus Christ protects our dreams and vision that will move forward our cause and that the enemy cannot manipulate these dreams and vision, in the name of Jesus Christ.

Isaiah 26: 9
My soul longs for thee in the night, and my spirit seeketh thee within me; for when thy judgments are made upon the earth, the inhabitants of the world learn righteousness.

B. IN THE MORNING
Apply the blood of Jesus Christ to prepare for your day.
We will use the blood of Jesus Christ to:

i) Purify our bodies, souls and spirits from all defilement that the devil and his agents have thrown on us during the night.

(ii) To cancel, annihilate, erase, remove, ...;
• All dreams and dreams sponsored by the Devil and his agents and all their consequences
• All plans, projects and orders by the devil and the authorities and principalities in the heavenly places.
• Any ambush and trap that the agents of darkness have stretched on roads, vehicles, places of work and schools where our children go to etc.

iii) Purify the air, water and any food we are going to consume throughout the day.

iv) Declare good things at the door of your day that you enter / begin your day with the accompaniment of all the blessings that the Lord God has promised us.

v) For the protection of your finances, cars, houses etc ... that the enemy does not have their hands on your property.

The word of God declares:
Job 38: 12-15
^{12} Since you have lived, "Have you ever given orders to the morning, or shown the dawn its place,
^{13} that it might take the earth by the edges and shake the wicked out of it?
^{14} The earth takes shape like clay under a seal; its features stand out like those of a garment.
^{15} The wicked are denied their light, and their upraised arm is broken.

22. I apply the blood of Jesus Christ to the door of this day (week, month ...) that Grace, favor, happiness, progress, health, good news and positive testimonies, accompany us in the Name of Jesus Christ of Nazareth.

23. May the blood of Jesus Christ overthrow and destroy all the traps, mystical cameras and cabalistic mirrors placed in the roads, the work places, in the schools of our children, in the name of Jesus Christ.

24. I plead the blood of Jesus Christ to cancel any accident or natural catastrophe planned by Satan and his agents in my life and my family in the name of Jesus Christ

25. This morning I drink the blood of Jesus Christ and cause my wife and all our children to drink the blood of Jesus Christ to repress all physical or spiritual food diabolically poisoned by the agents of darkness, in the name of Jesus Christ.

26. This morning I introduce the blood of Jesus Christ into my respiratory system, in that of my wife (husband) and our children, to block access to all poisoned air for the world of darkness and purify all that we will breathe in, in the name of Jesus Christ. The Word of God declares: Matthew 15:13 Every plant that my heavenly Father has not planted will be uprooted.

27. No misfortune happens to me. No scourge approaches my tent. For God commands his angels to keep me in all my ways. They carry me on my hands, lest my foot strike against a stone. Psalm 91: 10-12

28. I apply the blood of Jesus Christ in my body, soul and spirit to evacuate all diseases deposited upon me in dreams sponsored by the world of darkness, in the name of Jesus Christ.

29. Let the Blood of Jesus Christ erase my name, the name of my wife (my husband) and all our children, on mystical computers, on papers, on trees and on any evil site that agents of darkness used the night to condemn us, in the mighty name of Jesus Christ.

30. The word of God declares: But while the people were asleep, his enemy came and sowed tares among the wheat.

31. Let the blood of Jesus Christ purify and remove from our bodies every impurity that evil spirits have deposited at night while we slept.

32. Let the blood of Jesus Christ uproot and take away all tares sowed in our lives by men and women both physical and spiritual, in the name of Jesus Christ.

33. That the blood of Jesus Christ bring back into our lives all things that are stolen or exchanged during the night by the devil and his agents in the name of Jesus Christ.

34. Let the blood of Jesus Christ purifies the air that we are going to aspire from every kind of poison, both physical and spiritual, in the name of Jesus Christ.

35. In the name of Jesus Christ, let every physical or spiritual poison introduced or planified to be introduced into the food and drink that we are going to consume today, be evacuated and annihilated by the blood of Jesus Christ.

36. God instructs me for my good. He leads me in the way that I must follow. Isaiah 48:17

37. Let the blood of Jesus Christ precede us wherever we are going to put our feet on today, to annihilate and

remove all ambushes set by our enemies in the name of Jesus Christ.

38. I apply the blood of Jesus Christ to erase and break every pact, covenant, incantation and curses pronounced at night by the devil and his agents, in the name of Jesus Christ.

39. Every food I have eaten and every drink that I drank spiritually, consciously or unconsciously that gives access to the sorcerers in my life, I repay them with the blood of Jesus Christ.

40. The Word of God declares:
Isaiah 8:10
Devise your strategy, but it will be thwarted; propose your plan, but it will not stand, for God is with us.

41. By the power which is in the blood of Jesus Christ, I annihilate and render void and ineffectual all the programs devised by the enemy, all the projects of cunning men, and all incantations against me and my family, in the name of Jesus Christ.

42. I use the blood of Jesus Christ to prevent and destroy all the obstacles that the enemy has prepared for this day, in the name of Jesus Christ.

43. I apply the blood of Jesus Christ on the roads, parks, schools, jobs, to annihilate and destroy all the traps the enemy has set for us,

44. God overwhelms me with grace, and I lack nothing.
Genesis 33:11 .., **for God has been gracious to me and I have all I need."**

45. Lord God, I sprinkle the blood of Jesus Christ on all my body, soul and spirits, as well as everyone in my family, fill us with good by making all the work of our hands, the fruit of our flocks, and the fruit of our soil prosper; for you take pleasure in our happiness. Deuteronomy 30: 9

46. May the power of Jesus Christ's blood neutralize and evacuate all food prepared in the satanic kitchen that we had consumed in the name of Jesus Christ.

47. That any evil seed implanted in our lives or houses during the night for it to affect our way of life this morning, be uprooted by the blood of Jesus Christ.

48. Every seed of shame, every seed of poverty, every seed of rejection that the enemy has implanted in our lives during the night to disgrace us this day, be uprooted by the power of the blood of Jesus Christ.

49. Let the spirit of failure sent to accompany us this day, be swallowed up by the blood of Jesus Christ.

50. Let the blood of Jesus Christ break and ignite at night to make me step back or make me mark my steps in relation to my desired position in the name of Jesus Christ.

C. BEFORE CONSUMING ANY THING;

The Word of God declares:
1 Corinthians 10:31
Whether you eat, whether you drink, or do something else, do everything for the glory of God.

* After the actions of grace, apply the Blood of Jesus Christ to:
-Remove, evacuate and neutralize any object or substance that may be harmful to health.
-purify, sanctify your food
- protect sources of origin

D. THE BLOOD OF JESUS CHRIST IN EVERY DAY BATTLE.

A) Let us give thanks to the Lord God, for sending His only Son to die for us and to the Lord Jesus Christ for His Blood shed on the Cross for our cause.

The word of God declares; 1 Corinthians 6: 20
For you have been redeemed at a great price. So glorify God in your body and in your spirit, which belong to God.

51. O Lord God, we thank you and bless your holy name for your love for us; you have sent Jesus Christ to die on the cross for our salvation.

52. Father God, thank you for the work of the cross by which we are sanctified, justified and delivered by the blood of Jesus Christ.

53. Lord Jesus Christ, I bless you for your Blood, which has been shed for me and all my beloved ones, the Blood that redeemed us from the slavery of sin and made us free.

54. I praise you for your blood, which erases our condemnations and protects us day and night against any attack by the enemy.

55. Thank you Lord Jesus Christ for having agreed to die on the cross so that I and all my family will have victory over Satan and his followers.

56. Thank you Lord Jesus Christ for your Blood, that has delivered us from the works of Satan and his followers, and with your blood we have the assurance of walking in victory.

57. Thank you Lord Jesus Christ for your precious blood poured on the cross to give us life, security and hope of eternity.

58. Thank you Lord Jesus Christ for the work of the cross by which our sins are forgiven.

59. Thank you Lord Jesus Christ for the power of your Blood on our home. Amen.

B) Let us plead the Blood of Jesus Christ for the sanctification of our bodies, souls and spirits as well as all our goods.

The Word of God declares;
 Hebrews 9:22
And almost everything, according to the law, is purified with blood, and without shedding of blood there is no forgiveness.

60. I plead the Blood of Jesus Christ to wash us and to purify us in order to make us clean and spotless.

61. Let the precious blood of our Lord Jesus Christ shed on the cross for me and my household, sprinkle our bodies, souls and spirits to remove all that is unclean in us, in the mighty name of Jesus Christ.

62. Lord Jesus Christ, let your precious blood poured on the cross, purifies and sanctifies my body, soul and spirit, as well as my wife and children from all libations made in my name or my family.

63. Let the blood of Jesus Christ erase our transgressions, and wash us thoroughly of all our iniquities.

64. Let the Blood of Jesus Christ take away all that is sin in my body, soul and spirit.

65. May the Blood of Jesus Christ purify my tongue, my eyes and my ears, both physical and spiritual.

66. I sprinkle all my house with the Blood of Jesus Christ, to purify every object polluted by the devil and his agents, that the Blood of Jesus Christ purifies the water we drink, that the Blood of Jesus Christ purifies food That we eat, that the Blood of Jesus Christ purifies the clothes we bring and that the Blood of

Jesus Christ purifies the air we aspire to, in the mighty name of Jesus Christ.

67. May the blood of Jesus Christ sanctify, purify and justify all my children in the name of Jesus Christ.

68. I apply the Blood of Jesus Christ on all the doors and windows in my house, on utensils and furniture, on clothes and all other goods to sanctify them and purify them from any curse stuck on them.

69. The Word of God declares; **Colossians 2:14** having cancelled the charge of our legal indebtedness, which stood against us and condemned us; he has taken it away, nailing it to the cross.

70. Because the Lord Jesus Christ destroyed all the ordinances that condemned us, I come by the power that is in the blood of Jesus Christ to destroy all bonds and curses that have been established in our lives by heredity, in the name of Jesus Christ.

71. Let the blood of Jesus Christ annihilate all power behind the laws and ordinances that have been issued to torment my heart, in the name of Jesus Christ.

72. Lord Jesus Christ let your blood blot out any line drawn by the powers of darkness to limit my life or the life of my wife (my husband) and our children.

74. Let the Blood of Jesus Christ erase any anti-marriage mark on me that rejects the man (woman) of my life, in the name of Jesus Christ.

75. Any law contrary to the word of God assigned against my household be abolished by the blood of Jesus Christ, in the name of Jesus Christ.

76. I plead the blood of Jesus Christ to abrogate all established laws of my father's / mother's or in-laws' house which blocks fertility in any area in my home, in the name of Jesus Christ.

77. Let the Blood of Jesus Christ erase any mark of identification of the sorcerers that are upon me and that connects me to a person sent by the darkness for a painful relationship.

78. By the power of the Holy Spirit I plead the Blood of Jesus Christ to erase all ordinances from the condemnation that threatens my marriage (which keeps me in celibacy) in the name of Jesus Christ.

79. Lord Jesus Christ let your Blood erase every line drawn by the powers of darkness to limit my life in celibacy, in the name of Jesus Christ.

80. Let the Blood of Jesus Christ erase condemnations, decisions, etc., by prosecutors and magistrates of darkness, in the name of Jesus Christ.

81. Let every limit imposed in my life by the sorcery of my father's or mother's house be erased by the blood of Jesus Christ.

82. With the Blood of Jesus Christ, I break every hereditary curse of repeated failures, chronic celibacy, permanent poverty and premature death in my family, in the name of Jesus Christ.

83. Let the Blood of Jesus Christ erase all the curses placed upon me, my wife (husband) and all my children, as a result of the implications of the evil associations, my parents or ancestors, in the name of Jesus Christ.

84. I apply the Blood of Jesus Christ on my body, on my wife (my husband) and all our children to cleanse all signs of diabolical identification, in the name of Jesus Christ.

85. Lord God, let every evil tongue that utter curses and other evil declarations against my household be destroyed, and condemn it according to its own accusations, in the name of Jesus Christ.

86. I apply the blood of Jesus Christ on my body, soul and spirit as well as on my wife / husband and all our children to cancel all curses, incantations and bad luck which have been launched towards us, in the name of Jesus Christ.

D) Apply the Blood of Jesus Christ for your deliverance and that of your family

87. The word of God declares, Zechariah 9: 11-12: "And for thee, because of thy covenant sealed by the Blood, I will take captives out of the pit where there is no water."

88. Let the blood of our Lord Jesus Christ penetrate me deeply and deliver me from my faults, my anguish, my bitterness, and all the wounds of the Heart.

89. Let the Blood of Jesus Christ deliver me from all enchantment, all bewitchment and all evil influence of the living or the dead, exercised by Erotic dreams or nightmares, in the name of Jesus Christ of Nazareth.

90. Let that the blood of Jesus Christ frees us (me and my family) from all forms of magic, witchcraft and sorcery transmitted through us by my father's house or by my mother's house in the name of Jesus Christ of Nazareth.

91. I plead the blood of Jesus Christ in my life and in all my family to annihilate all the forces behind all the habits and ways of life associated with family or territorial altars in the name of Jesus Christ.

92. Let the Blood of Jesus Christ erase all the names of the gods invoked in my father's house and in my mother's house, and that the power behind these names becomes null and void in the name of Jesus Christ.

93. Let every seat of witchcraft implanted in my house, in my workplace, in my ministry, in my family, etc., be unveiled and carried away by the blood of Jesus Christ, in the name of Jesus Christ.

94. You, the agent of the devil who sucks the blood of any person in my family, I present to you the blood of Jesus Christ, that every drop of sucked blood be vomited now in the name of Jesus Christ.

95. Lord God! May the blood of Jesus Christ detach our bonds because we are your servants.

96. Every obstacle places on the road of my breakthrough be taken away by the blood of Jesus Christ, in the name of Jesus Christ.

97. Let the blood of Jesus Christ remove any mark of wizard identification that is on me or on any member of my family and on all our possessions, in the name of Jesus Christ.

98. You witchcraft, who swallowed my job, my health, my marriage, etc ... vomit it now, in the name of Jesus Christ.

99. Every bank and fortress of witchcraft which harbor my blessings and treasures be inundated with the blood of Jesus Christ, in the name of Jesus Christ.

100. I drink the blood of Jesus Christ and have my wife and children drink, to evacuate all satanic meat, eaten physically or spiritually, and which is found in our bodies in the name of Jesus Christ.

101. I apply the blood of Jesus Christ to erase and eliminate our names on altars, mystical computers, on trees, on cemeteries, etc ... that the devil uses to continue to demand and condemn us in the name of Jesus Christ.

102. Let the blood of Jesus Christ speaks for my family and let it fight for us visible and invisible fighting, in the name of Jesus Christ.

103. I plead the blood of Jesus Christ to erase all written or verbal words against my life or that of my wife (husband) and our children, in the mighty name of Jesus Christ.

104. Let the Blood of Jesus Christ deliver us from all enchantment, all bewitchment and all evil influence of the living or the dead affecting my life, that of my wife (husband) and all our children, in the name of Jesus Christ.

105. Let the blood of Jesus Christ shut up all doors which I opened myself to the enemy.

106. Every embargo imposed upon me by the sorcery of my father's or mother's house be carried away by the Blood of Jesus Christ.

107. I apply the blood of Jesus Christ in my body, soul and spirit to remove the mask of old age that distances the man (woman) whom God has planned for me,

108. I apply the blood of Jesus Christ in my body, soul and spirit to wash and remove any evil smell that repels the man (woman) whom God has planned for me.

109. Let the Blood of Jesus Christ break every curse and the covenant of solitude by the house of my father / mother, in the name of Jesus Christ.

110. Let the blood of Jesus Christ remove on my path any spirit, any person blocking the way to my destiny and confiscates my possessions, in the name of Jesus Christ.

111. Let the blood of Jesus Christ neutralize and break the spirit of anger which the enemy implanted in me or whom I inherited from my father's house or from my mother's house, in the name of Jesus Christ.

112. Let the blood of Jesus Christ destroy all spirit of retardation in my life, in my mind, in the life of my wife (my husband) and my children, in the name of Jesus Christ.

113. Let the blood of Jesus Christ blindly strikes any unwholesome spirit or any creature seeking to locate our blessings, in the name of Jesus Christ.

114. You, evil tree implanted in the centre of my home by anyone with a mission to produce rebellion, quarrels and quarrels, discordance, be shaken by the Blood of Jesus Christ.

115. By the power that is in the Blood of Jesus Christ, I overthrow every family altar used to torment my marriage in the name of Jesus Christ.

116. That the blood of Jesus Christ erases any satanic mark on our bodies that connect us with the world of darkness, in the name of Jesus Christ.

E) Use the Blood of Jesus Christ to pay the debts accumulated by you consciously or unconsciously. The Blood of Jesus Christ to pay the debts accumulated by our parents and ancestors and that the creditor "the enemy" claims until today

117. Satan and your demons, I present to you the Blood of Jesus Christ as payment for all debts known and unknown that you cease to claim on my marriage / home, in the mighty name of Jesus Christ.

118. Lord Jesus Christ, let your blood shed on the cross erase all curses and condemnations resulting from the debts accumulated by our parents or our ancestors, in the name of Jesus Christ.

119. I plead the Blood of Jesus Christ to pay the debts both physical and spiritual accumulated by our parents or ancestors and which the enemy claims until today, in the name of Jesus Christ.

120. I plead the Blood of Jesus Christ to pay for the spiritual debts accumulated by me voluntarily or involuntarily, in the name of Jesus Christ

121. I apply the Blood of Jesus Christ to reimburse any object or money that someone with bad intentions has contributed to my life, my wedding day, my journey and my business, in the name of Jesus Christ.

F) Apply the blood of Jesus Christ in all areas of your life where there is a bad foundation.

122. I plead the Blood of Jesus Christ on all evil practices done and any evil words spoken before, during and after my birth that connects me with the world of darkness, let the Blood of Jesus Christ annihilate the power behind this foundation, in the name of Jesus Christ.

123. Let the Blood of Jesus Christ carry away every object, every word that represents partially or wholly an evil foundation in my marriage, in the name of Jesus Christ.

124. I plead the blood of Jesus Christ on all parts of my physical body, to break every mysterious object or animal by agents of darkness in the name of Jesus Christ.

125. Let the Blood of Jesus Christ break every curse resulting from an evil foundation in my marriage in the name of Jesus Christ.

126. Every force, every power of darkness supporting evil foundations in my marriage, be destroyed and be broken, in the name of Jesus Christ.

127. Let the blood of Jesus Christ stop and break any demonic activity planned on the family altars that happens in my house in the name of Jesus Christ.

128. I apply the Blood of Jesus Christ in my life and in the lives of every person in my family to erase all curses and condemnations resulting from demonic activities on family and territorial altars, in the name of Jesus Christ.

129. I apply the Blood of Jesus Christ on my physical and spiritual life, as well as on that of my wife (husband) and all our children, to erase and break any curse of sexual immorality resulting from incest, lesbianism, Homosexuality, bestiality, fornication, adultery, oral sex and abortions and all the sins and sexual iniquities of our parents, in the name of Jesus Christ of Nazareth.

130. I apply the Blood of Jesus Christ to erase all points of limitation decided on the family altars, in the mighty name of Jesus Christ.

131. By the power which is in the blood of our Lord Jesus Christ, I now annul all covenants, all vows, and pacts made with the devil on the family or territorial altars, either by my ancestors or by the authorities both political and academic, for controlling, directing or frustrating our lives, in the name of Jesus Christ.

132. Let the Blood of Jesus Christ breaks and disconnects from my home, every spirit of polygamy, every spirit of incest nourished by the witchcraft of my

father / mother's or in-law's house, in the name of Jesus Christ.

133. Let the Blood of Jesus Christ cancel and erase any blood covenant made by myself, my parents or ancestors with the world of darkness, in the name of Jesus Christ.

134. Lord Jesus Christ, let your blood penetrate into the body of each of my children and replace the blood of the family line of condemnation, in the name of Jesus Christ.

135. Let the Blood of Jesus Christ block any gateway to sorcery and poverty in my life, in the life of my wife and children, in the name of Jesus Christ.

G) Apply the Blood of Jesus Christ on your life and that of your loved ones as well as all your goods and interests to be protected against Satan and his acolytes (demons, magicians, sorcerers and witches, occultists)

136. The Word of God declares; Exodus 12:13 The blood shall serve you as a sign upon the houses where you are; I will see the blood, and I will pass over you, and there will be no plague which will destroy you, when I strike the land of Egypt.

137. Like the blood of the lambs with which the gates of the Hebrews were sprinkled, which removed the

exterminating angel, so that the mighty blood of Jesus Christ, fearful to the unclean spirits, filled them with terror and removed them from me and my home Name of Jesus Christ.

138. In the mighty name of Jesus Christ, I come to cover my household and all our goods with the blood of Jesus Christ.

139. I apply the Blood of Jesus Christ on me and on the life of every person in my family, to make us invisible and unassailable to the eyes and attacks of the enemy, in the mighty name of Jesus Christ.

140. The Word of God declares:
Joshua 2:18 "When we enter into the land, tie this cord of crimson thread to the window by which you bring us down, and gather with you in the house your father, your mother, your brothers, and all the family of your father. "

141. I cover my home, my marriage, my wife (my husband) with the blood of our Lord Jesus Christ, to drive away all bewitchment, all enchantment and all manipulation of the world of darkness.

142. Let the Blood of Jesus Christ form a river around my life and my home and all our goods, in order swallow up and destroy every spirit sent by the darkness to do us harm, in the name of Jesus Christ.

143. I introduce my life, that of my wife (husband) and of each of our children and all our possessions into the Blood of Jesus Christ in order to prevent agents of darkness from locating us, in the name of Jesus Christ.

144. I apply the Blood of Jesus Christ throughout my home to secure my marriage, to protect me and my partner against any planned attack by my father's / mother's or in-law's house, any ill-intentioned person, in the name of Jesus Christ.

145. The Word of God declares:
Psalms 35: 1-2
¹ Contend, LORD, with those who contend with me;
 fight against those who fight against me.
² Take up shield and armour; arise and come to my aid.

146. Let the Blood of Jesus Christ fight for us all the battles visible as invisible, in the name of Jesus Christ.

147. I cover our lives and all our possessions with the Blood of Jesus Christ to protect us from all evil plans against us and I render void and ineffectual all the projects and decisions that Satanists make against us, in the name of Jesus Christ.

148. I apply the blood of Jesus Christ on the roads, parks, schools, and jobs to protect us from attacks of the enemy.

149. I apply the Blood of Jesus Christ to my life, to the life of a woman (my husband), and to all our

children as brands, to repel every wind, every temptation and every agent of the devil and send them far from us, in the name of Jesus Christ.

150. I sprinkle the Blood of Jesus Christ in my house, on the doors, on the windows, on the beds and on the utensils that we use, to swallow up every power and every spirit left by the devil with the mission to control us, in the name of Jesus Christ.

151. Lord Jesus Christ let your Blood swallow up all the fiery arrow of the enemy that is cast towards us, in the name of Jesus Christ.

152. Let the blood of Jesus Christ break all communication and contact between my home and the mystical world, the parallel world or the pandemonium world, in the name of Jesus Christ.

153. I apply the blood of Jesus Christ around my marriage, to make us invisible and unassailable to the eyes and attacks of all our enemies.

154. I cover all my family with the blood of Jesus Christ, lord when your anger will strike the wicked, see the blood of Jesus Christ on my home, on all my family and let no wound destroy us , Protect us, oh Lord, our God.

155. I apply the Blood of Jesus Christ on every door, on every the window, on the beds, on the furniture,

utensils and on all our clothes, that the devil and his demons cannot use these objects to attack us.

156. When I walk in the valley of the shadow of death, I fear no evil, for the LORD is with me. (Psalms 23: 4)

157. The LORD protects me in his tabernacle in the day of misfortune, he hides me under the shelter of his tent. He raises me on a rock. Psalms 27: 5

158. For the LORD loves the just, and he does not forsake his faithful one; they are always under his guard, Wrongdoers will be completely destroyed; the offspring of the wicked will perish.Psalms 37: 28

159. The word of God declares, But God will redeem me from the realm of the dead; he will surely take me to himself (Psalms 49:15)
I plead, therefore, that the blood of Jesus Christ always keep me under the guard of God, and that he will cut off all the wicked and their posterity among us, in the name of Jesus Christ.

160. The Word of God declares:
Then all that trust in thee shall rejoice; they shall rejoice forever, and thou shalt protect them; you will be a subject of joy for those who love your name.

164. Let the blood of Jesus Christ block every gateway to sorcery and poverty in my life, in the life of my wife

(my husband) and all our children, in the name of Jesus Christ.

165. Let the blood of Jesus Christ shut down any door that I, my wife (my husband) or my children have opened to Satan and his agents, in the name of Jesus Christ.

166. Let the blood of Jesus Christ form a barrier between us and all our enemies, that they won't be able to see or touch our lives and possessions, in the name of Jesus Christ.

H) Apply the Blood of Jesus Christ for the healing and recovery of our bodies, souls and spirits.

The Word of God declares: Isaiah 53: 5 But he was wounded for our sins, Broken for our iniquities; the punishment which gives us peace has fallen upon him, and it is through his stripes that we are healed.

167. 1 Peter 2:24 "He himself bore our sins" in his body on the cross, so that we might die to sins and live for righteousness; "by his wounds you have been healed."

168. I drink the blood of Jesus Christ, I cause my wife and all our children to drink the blood of Jesus Christ to purify every organ of our bodies (quote the organ if you know which one is sick), to wash out hidden disease, in the name of Jesus Christ.

169. Let the blood of Jesus Christ strengthen every organ of my body weakened by Satan and his agents.

170. Let any hereditary disease declared at the family altar be stopped by the blood of Jesus Christ.

171. Let any demonic object implanted in my blood system be evacuated by the blood of Jesus Christ.

172. The spirit of infirmity affecting any area of my life, or that of my wife and children, be engulfed, in the blood of Jesus Christ.

173. Let any genetic disease in the family line from my father's side, from my mother's side or from my in-laws, affecting my children, be burned by God's fire and be evacuated from their bodies by the blood of Jesus Christ.

174. Let the blood of Jesus Christ neutralizes and eliminates from my life, from my wife (my husband) and from the life of one of each child, from every poison of the serpent, scorpion or other reptile that the agents of Darkness use to infect us physically or spiritually, in the name of Jesus Christ.

175. By the power of the Holy Spirit, I introduce the Blood of Jesus Christ into my blood system, that of my wife (husband), and all our children to annihilate and stop all the negative effects caused by diabolical transfusions.

176. Let the blood of Jesus Christ restore life to every organ of our bodies, where the devil and his agents injected the sickness, let it be healed, wherever they brought death, let life regain, In the name of Jesus Christ.

177. Lord God, remove sickness from me, remove sickness from my wife (my husband) and all our children, in the name of Jesus Christ. Exodus 23:25

178. By the power which is in the blood of Jesus Christ, I declare that every anomaly in my body, in the body of my wife and in the body of each of my children be corrected to the normal, in the name of Jesus Christ.

I) The word of GOD DECLARES: "Life is in the blood" (Leviticus 17:11).
The precious Blood of Jesus Christ is for Christians the key that opens the door to all the physical and spiritual blessings that God has given us in Christ.

179. Let the blood of Jesus Christ opens all doors of our blessings blocked by the powers of the world of darkness, in the name of Jesus Christ.

180. Thus, by the love of our Lord God, according to his promise in Genesis 17: 7, I present the Blood of Jesus Christ as a sacrifice that will speak eternally in our favor on our altars.

181. Let the Blood of Jesus Christ blocks every gateway to sorcery and poverty in my life, in the life of my wife (my husband) and all our children in the mighty name of Jesus Christ.

182. Let the Blood of Jesus Christ speak for my family and fight for us visible and invisible battles.

183. Let the Blood of Jesus Christ sweep away all altars of sorcery and poverty from my father's house and from my mother's house, in the name of Jesus Christ.

184. Let the Blood of Jesus Christ erase any line drawn by the powers of darkness to limit my life or that of my wife (my husband) and all our children, in the name of Jesus Christ.

185. I apply the Blood of Jesus Christ in my life, in the life of my wife (husband) and all our children, in order to show the mark of favor that the Lord Jesus Christ accords according to His grace to accompany us in all the rest of our journey on earth, in the name of Jesus Christ.

The Blood of Jesus Christ

186. The Word of God declares;
Galatians 6:17
From now on, let no one cause me trouble, for I bear on my body the marks of Jesus..

187. That the Blood of Jesus Christ uproots every evil seed implanted in the life of each of my children by the agents of darkness in the name of Jesus Christ.

188. Every object implanted in my house or in the bodies of my children to facilitate communication with the world of darkness, be evacuated by the blood of Jesus Christ. Every trap or conspiracy against my elevation is annihilated by the blood of Jesus Christ.

189. Every trap or conspiracy against my elevation be annihilated by the blood of Jesus Christ.

190. Let all strong men and strong women executing orders from my father's and my mother's house, be weakened and swallowed up by the blood of Jesus Christ.

191. Let the blood of Jesus Christ restore any couple that is threatened with separation or divorce, in the name of Jesus Christ.

193. Let the power of the cross of our Lord Jesus Christ accompany all labor of our hands and of our intelligence, in the name of Jesus Christ.

The Blood of Jesus Christ

194. The Word of God declares; Genesis 17: 7
I will establish my covenant as an everlasting covenant between me and you and your descendants after you for the generations to come, to be your God and the God of your descendants after you.

195. By the power of the Holy Spirit, I come to erect a new altar for my life and my entire household, an altar founded on the death and resurrection of our Lord Jesus Christ.

196. I plead the blood of Jesus Christ to bring back to me and my family all good things that we had lost.

197. I plead the blood of Jesus Christ to close any door that I opened to Satan consciously or unconsciously in the name of Jesus Christ.

198. Let the blood of Jesus Christ shut down any entrance door opened by my parents or ancestors, in the mighty name of Jesus Christ.

199. I plead the blood of Jesus Christ against any satanic maneuver seeking to bring distraction into my home, in the name of Jesus Christ.

200. God, Let the blood of Jesus Christ sprinkle our bodies, souls and spirits with blessings that will make us prosper in all that we are going to undertake, in the name of Jesus Christ.

201. The Word of God declares; all that you will bind on earth will be bound in heaven, let the blood of Jesus Christ encircle all the fortresses of the enemy that host our finances, in the name of Jesus Christ.

202. The Word of God declares; what you will loose on earth will be loosed in heaven, let the blood of Jesus Christ locate and free our health and our finances, in the mighty name of Jesus Christ.

203. O Lord God, I plead the blood of Jesus Christ to wash and remove from our memories everything that the enemy uses to veil us and prevent us from seeing what you have reserved for us, in the name of Jesus Christ.

204. The word of God says (Psalm 91: 10 no harm will overtake you, no disaster will come near your tent. Thus, God, let the blood of Jesus Christ forms a barrage all around my life, around my Home and everything in our house, in the name of Jesus Christ.

205. By the power of the Holy Spirit, I declare that the blood of Jesus Christ transform;
* any defeat that we had suffered in our dreams in victory, in the name of Jesus Christ.
* Any failure the enemy has inflicted in our lives in success.
* All our points of weakness in strong points
* the curses which the devil and his agents have pronounced upon us in blessings.

* Sadness in joy.
* Diseases in good health.
* Limitations and slavery in freedom.
* All financial losses programmed by the devil and his agents in profits.

206. I plead the blood of Jesus Christ against;
-the spirit of vagrancy in my family, in the name of Jesus Christ.
- the spirit of delay in my life and everyone in my home, in the name of Jesus Christ.
-The spirit of sterility in every domain of my life, in the name of Jesus Christ.
Swallowers of our finances, in the name of Jesus Christ.
-any spirit of derivation in the name of Jesus Christ.

-All satanic prophecy for my family, in the name of Jesus Christ.

207. Let the power of the resurrection of our Lord Jesus Christ accompany all labor of my hands, of my understanding, and of my wife and children, in the name of Jesus Christ.

208. Let the blood of Jesus Christ open all doors of my blessings blocked by the powers of the world of darkness, in the name of Jesus Christ.

209. Since Jesus Christ has freed the captives, I declare the total liberation of our bodies and souls, in the name of Jesus Christ.

210. Let the blood of Jesus Christ revives all that was struck or threatened with death or destruction around me, in the name of Jesus Christ.

J) Seal your prayer with the blood of Jesus Christ.

The word of God declares;

Exodus 12: 22-23

²² Take a bunch of hyssop, dip it into the blood in the basin and put some of the blood on the top and on both sides of the doorframe. None of you shall go out of the door of your house until morning. ²³ When the LORD goes through the land to strike down the Egyptians, he will see the blood on the top and sides of the doorframe and will pass over that doorway, and he will not permit the destroyer to enter your houses and strike you down.

211. Let the power of the resurrection of our Lord Jesus Christ be on the work of our hands to protect our careers and that the blood of Jesus Christ block any opening that gives or will give Satan and his agents the

opportunity To act in our lives and our children, in the name of Jesus Christ.

212. I cover my life and that of every one in my family and all our possessions by the blood of Jesus Christ, to make us invisible and unassailable to the eyes and the attacks of the world of darkness

213. I encircle all my family and all our blessings with the blood of Jesus Christ. Henceforth no power of darkness will come near and operate from our homes, in the name of Jesus Christ.

214. I now apply the Blood of Jesus Christ on my body, on my soul and on my mind, and around all my interests to create a forbidden zone for all evil spirits seeking to reach me, in the name of Jesus Christ.

215. Lord Jesus Christ, I thank you for the marvelous work which you have accomplished on the cross, through which you have stripped dominions and authorities and have publicly delivered us by triumphing over them on the cross.

216. Lord Jesus Christ I thank you, for your powerful hand of the deliverance that you have just accomplished in my home, thank you for your presence among us.

217. God, I believe in your word, and I know that what you promised in your word is always fulfilled, for it is written: all that you ask in prayer believe that you have received it and you Will see fulfillment (Mark 11:24)

218. Thank you, Lord Jesus Christ, for your assurance that your blood will protect us from all evil, danger and temptation, for we believe in what the Bible declares; Let no man hurt me now, for I bear on my body the mark of Jesus Christ. (Galatians 6:17)

219. I here seal my prayer by the Blood of Jesus Christ that the devil and his agents cannot decipher, steal or block our requests, in the mighty name of Jesus Christ.

220. Thank you Lord Jesus Christ for the wonderful benefits that Your Blood gives me. Because your blood has been shed for me, I am redeemed, I am delivered from my sins, justified, purified, sanctified and set aside for God

Benediction and Final Greetings

[20] Now may the God of peace, who through the blood of the eternal covenant brought back from the dead our Lord Jesus, that great Shepherd of the sheep,
[21] equip you with everything good for doing his will, and may he work in us what is pleasing to him, through Jesus Christ, to whom be glory forever and ever.
(Hebrews 13: 20-21)

WE HAVE SO PRAYED AND ALL WE SAY; AMEN!

RADIO PLANET BEREE
RADIO CHRETIENNE

Live 24/7

www.planetberee.com

planetberee@gmail.com

youtube : Planet beree

Facebook : planetberee

The Blood of Jesus Christ

Made in the USA
Middletown, DE
02 June 2025

76458828R00038